CLARA

The True Story of Clara the Rhino,
an Eighteenth Century Superstar!

For my wonderful Mum

Second Edition published 2020
First published in Great Britain in 2016 by Books By Sarah Publishing
Text and illustrations copyright © Sarah Hewitt 2016
ISBN 9781539669791
The right of Sarah Hewitt to be identified as the Author and Illustrator of The Work has been asserted by her
in accordance with the Copyright, Design and Patents Act of 1988. All rghts reserved.
No part of this publication may be reproduced, stored in a retrieval system, or transmitted, in any form, or by any means,
electrical, mechanical, photocopying, recording or otherwise without prior permission of the publisher
or a licence permissing restricted copying.
In the United Kingdom such licences are issued by the Copyright Licensing Agency,
Barnard's Inn, 86 Fetter Lane, London EC4A 1EN

CLARA

Written and illustrated by Sarah Hewitt

This is the true story about the amazing adventures of an Indian rhino called Clara.

Clara was born in a country called India.
She lived in the jungle with her mum and it was peaceful and beautiful.

One sad day, hunters came to the jungle.
Clara and her mum were scared and they ran away.

Clara went to hide but she got lost.
She felt very sad and alone.

When the hunters found her, poor Clara was very afraid. She really missed her mum.

Clara wondered what was going to happen next...

She arrived at a beautiful palace.
The kind family who lived there said they would buy Clara.

The family loved her straight away. Clara was safe and she didn't feel quite so sad anymore.

Time passed.

But every day Clara grew bigger....

...and bigger

...and bigger!

The family were very worried because Clara was too big for the palace. "What shall we do?" they wondered...

A sea captain said he would take care of her.
Clara felt sad again. What will happen now she thought...

Clara was put onto a huge ship. The Captain talked to her kindly and gave her lots of nice food.

On and on they sailed, for thousands of miles until they reached a country called Holland.

Clara and the Captain became good friends.

One day the Captain had a surprise for Clara.
"Let's go on an adventure!" he said...

Clara and the Captain rode across the countryside in a huge carriage pulled by eight horses.

They journeyed far away, to places where no one had ever seen a rhino before....

...they travelled far and wide to many countries and even met kings and queens....

.....and everywhere they went, people cheered for Clara!
"Hurray for Clara, the Superstar!"

Clara was so famous an artist painted her portrait!

"Hurray for Clara, the Superstar!"

Many years have passed since the Captain and Clara made their amazing journey but even now, people still go to see the portrait of Clara,

"The rhino who travelled the world!"

"Hurray for Clara, the Superstar!"

From the Author:

Thank you for reading 'Clara'. I hope she made you smile.
Please leave me a review on Amazon.

To learn about more of my books or to send me a messsage,
please visit my website at www.booksbysarah.co.uk

Printed in Great Britain
by Amazon